From Busy to Rich

Forward by Pastor Rob Koke

Wesley Young

Table of Contents

-Spending Blueprint Quick Start Guide

"A practical approach that brings more meaning to living a rich and faithful life. Wes utilizes key Biblical principles to help illustrate how our misconceptions of being rich will actually defeat God's true intentions for our lives. Creating more than you consume is a powerful and fundamental principle that everyone can learn."

Warburg Lee

CEO, Alen Corp.

"Wes Young is a visionary and a tremendous motivator. This book will show you God's plan for being rich and the steps you need to take to get there. You will also come away with a lot of quality nuggets and quotes that you will want to jot down. I highly recommend this book to anyone who wants to improve their quality of life."

Ron Brigmon

President, Ron Brigmon Ministries, Inc.

"This is a book that I will be sharing with family, friends, and associates. I love the concept of the book, and believe it can have a strong impact in the lives of those who practice the principles outlined."

Eric B Campbell

Managing Partner,

New York Life Insurance Company

"Wes Young has written an excellent book that takes a fresh and innovative look at some our most common and treasured myths surrounding the whole concept of growth, wealth and success. With out being preachy he takes timeless truths and presents them with practical insight to unveil what being truly rich is all about."

Robert J Koke

Senior Pastor, Shoreline Church

"As a life long entrepreneur, I wish I could have had this book decades ago. I know of no substitute for the powerful principals Wes shares in "From Busy to Rich". If you are a business owner seeking to unlock extra time and money, you hold in your hand the key."

Jim Pendleton

Owner, Eads-Pendleton

"Wes delivers great insight on what it means to be wealthy. Life's "tension" helps really put into perspective our struggle to fit the reality of our earthly dominion calling in this fallen world with God's promises of our Heavenly possessions"

Clay Carter

Financial Advisor -Carter Wealth Management

To book Wes for church, corporate events

or workshops call: 512-329-4286

For more information go to:

www.WesleyYoung.com

Forward

True success is really difficult to measure. There are so many different definitions. And many of the most popular ones are at best misleading and hard to wrap your understanding around. This is especially true when it involves coming to grips with your finances. We ask ourselves questions. What is "financial success"? What should my goals be? What do we do with distance between where I am now and where I want to go? What practical habits and attitudes should define my approach to wealth?

Wes Young has written an excellent book that takes a fresh and innovative look at some our most common and treasured myths surrounding the whole concept of growth, wealth and success. With out being preachy he takes timeless truths and presents them with practical insight to unveil what being truly rich is all about. I loved his home-spun stories and practical insight and so will you. Find your favorite reading spot and make sure you have a pen to underline what speaks to you and enjoy the journey "From Busy to Rich"!

Robert J Koke

Senior Pastor Shoreline Church

Introduction

M any great men and women spend a ton of effort running fast and working hard to get to the place of more than enough. They are the entrepreneurs who make a lot of money but have no liquidity. The only governing limit to their spending is when the money (or credit) runs out. The one thing that never runs out, however, is the next idea they are trying to get done. If they can just capture that next idea, then they can have the rest and margin that comes with being rich. Therefore, the key to being rich in their mind must be to run faster and work harder. The problem is they never find what they are looking for running at this unsustainable pace, they just end up tired and broke. They have been pursuing a destination that doesn't exist.

Ever feel like you run out of money before you run out of all the ideas and opportunities you want to pursue? Does extra time and extra money seem like a mirage that continues to elude you? Join Wes Young as he unpacks the topic of what it really means to be rich. In this book, we will discover why continuing to try to out earn or out run all your ideas will never leave you the extra time and extra money you are looking for. We will unpack the real definition of being rich and the fundamentals that we need to create more than we consume on a consistent basis. Whether you desire to be wealthier or if you just want to fine-tune your moneymaking ability, this book will help you unlock the thinking required to do it. You will also learn how to get out of debt and create the extra time and extra money that you seek, without compromising God's vision for your life. **BEING RICH IS GOD'S IDEA.** In Proverbs 10:22, Solomon, the richest man to ever live said, "The blessing of the Lord makes one rich, and He adds no sorrow to it." Let's learn how to receive those blessings! Let's see what God's idea of Being Rich is all about!

Part 1 – "Redefining Rich"

A Destination That Does Not Exist

In the hot West Texas town of Odessa, if you wanted to go fishing, you were going to be driving because the closest lakes were about three hours by car. So that's what we did. I was fifteen years old when my sister Mandy (who was twenty) and her boyfriend, Mark, and I all loaded up in my mom's red Ford Probe and headed for the lake they called Big Lake. We chose Big Lake because it was one of the closer lakes to us based on my parents giant State Farm Atlas (an atlas for those of you who don't know was a book of maps that we used to get to our destination pre GPS days). After about a three-hour drive we arrived in the town of Big Lake and took a right according to the atlas's instructions. From the mileage scale it looked like the lake was about five miles outside of town. As we hit mile five, we eagerly anticipated the glistening lake that would appear over one of the upcoming rolling hills. That anticipation turned into confusion and finally frustration as the miles ticked by with no lake to be seen. It was about mile twenty that my sister's boyfriend, Mark (who would later become my brother-in-law), stopped the car and grabbed the atlas out of my hands in anger (sure I had taken us off course somehow). About an hour later of driving around, yelling at each other, and all of us taking turns staring at the same State Farm Atlas, we found ourselves at a gas station parking lot in the town of Big Lake waiting for Mark to come back out with directions from a local. As he got back in the car and sat down, my sister and I looked at him with a suggestive, "well?" Then he said something none of us expected. "It doesn't exist!" We said, "What do you mean it doesn't exist? It's right here on the atlas;

the town is even named Big Lake." Mark's reply was, "The manager of the gas station said the lake dried up about ten years ago; the atlas is out of date; the lake doesn't exist." That was the day we all learned there is nothing quite as frustrating as searching for a destination that does not exist.

As frustrating as it was at the time, that story has become one of our favorites around Thanksgiving dinner. It has also become a great reminder to me of a fundamental truth, "there is nothing more frustrating than spending your time, energy and money searching for a destination that does not exist." **When it comes to the idea of being rich most people spend their lives in pursuit of a destination that does not exist.** In this short book, it is my desire to help root out and pull down the false assumptions people live under when it comes to being rich, then to build and plant a foundational perspective that will unlock your true ability to be rich.

A Bad Definition

Ask any group of honest people if they want to be rich and the answer they will give is going to be yes. Critics may say being rich doesn't make you happy, but the truth is if they were given a choice between being unhappy and rich and unhappy and not rich, I think they would choose unhappy and rich. As one man put it, "Being rich is not the key to happiness, but if you're rich enough you can have a key made." All kidding aside, here is the interesting thing: though everyone would like to be rich and many people spend an enormous part of their lives trying to be rich, very few people have ever taken the time to define what it actually means to them to be rich. Think about it for a minute. What do you think it means to be rich? Though most of us have never taken the time to formally define it, I would submit that we all have at least a subconscious definition that moves us to action in our attempt to be rich. In fact, when you really take the time to look at the actions of those of us in pursuit of being rich a clear definition emerges. **Most people define being rich as getting to the place where you have more money than ideas.** Being rich, for most, means arriving at the destination that we have out earned our wants. That is why the primary pursuit in our culture is to run faster and work harder, to fit more into our already overcrowded schedules in an attempt to outrun our ideas. Because in the final internal (and I believe subconscious) analysis, most people think the key to having extra time and extra money is to run faster and work harder in order to out run or out earn their ideas. **The problem with that definition of being rich is, it is not only a bad definition, it is an impossible one. That's not how to be rich, that's how to be busy and tired. The reason it is an impossible definition to achieve is due to one undeniable truth, all of us**

will run out of time and money before we run out of ideas and opportunities we want to pursue.

The Gap

The reason that all of us will run out of time and money before we run out of ideas and opportunities is simple, all of us have a gap between what we see and what could be. And no matter how much you earn and how fast you run that gap doesn't go away, it just moves. Think about it with me for a second. Think back to the first job you got a paycheck for. Mine was in a Blockbuster Video and my role was to put the tapes (that's right TAPES) back on the shelves when they came in. I was 15 and I was making $4.25 an hour, which was the minimum wage at the time. I don't know what your first job was, but I'll bet somewhere in that first year of work you had the same thought about money that I had, "When I am just making a little bit more money, then I am going to be rich." In fact, when we would look at people that were two or three income levels above us, we couldn't help but wonder why they seem so stressed out financially, because in our eyes they should have more than enough. They should have been throwing a party they had so much more than we did. The reason I believed this was the same reason you did. I had a gap that existed between what I could see today and what could be tomorrow. And, at fifteen, the gap wasn't all that big. Another dollar an hour would get everything accomplished to get me to the other side of that gap, with some to spare. Essentially, all I had to do was out earn my gap, and then I would be rich, right? Well as you could probably guess, **years later I was making a lot more money and the gap hadn't gone away, it had just moved**. Certainly I had captured many of the things that made up the gap between what I could see and what could be, but as I did, new pursuits just replaced the old ones. It is so strange that even though you continue to make more and more money, you just never seem to arrive at that place of more than enough.

If any of this is starting to sound familiar to you, you are not alone. In fact, the Gallup organization did a study that I believe clearly reveals this sub-conscious definition that rests in the heart of the majority. Here were the results of Gallup's survey of over 11,000 people who were asked, "What does it take to be rich?" Income earners who made $30,000 and less, said it would take an annual income of $74,000 to be rich. Now for those of you who make $74,000 per year you are saying to yourself, I may not know what rich is exactly, but I can tell you it isn't $74,000. Because you still have house payments, and car payments and there is not a whole lot of extra to go around right? Well you are not alone in your thinking because look how the answers changed as they went up to the next level of income. Income earners, who made between $30,000 and $50,000, said it took $100,000 of annual income to be rich. Once again, if you make a $100,000 per year your likely response is, that is not rich! And once again you would not be alone in your thinking. As you go through the study this trend continues. For the overwhelming majority of participants, rich was always more than they currently made! Though the numbers may change, there is one popular idea that boils to the top, "To be rich I need more than I currently have!" Funny isn't it? Though people may have disagreed on the amount of money it took to be rich, one thing they were unanimous about was that it was going to take more than they currently had. The reason? **All of us have a gap between what we see and what could be. That gap never goes away it just moves. So if your strategy for being rich is to try to out run or out earn that gap, not only is that a bad strategy, but also it is an**

impossible one. That is not a recipe for rich; it's a recipe for busy and tired.

Here is the point where I know what some of you are thinking, "But what about the really rich people, can't they out earn and out run their ideas?" Let me give you some examples that will help us here. I am a financial advisor to people that own businesses and real estate. I have a client, in his eighties, who is worth about $275,000,000. I remember visiting with him one day on the reality that all of us will run out of time and money before we will run out of ideas and opportunities we want to pursue. Here is what he told me, "Wes, see that airplane over there (pointing to his 16 million dollar airplane)? I dreamed about that for years and I am grateful that God has blessed me to have it, but you know what? The one I really want is this 50 million dollar air plane (showing me a picture on the internet). What amazes me is I remember when all I wanted was a 400 dollar car. It's a funny thing Wes, I am grateful for what I have, but getting it does not quench the ideas I have for what could be next." I have had countless discussions with some of the wealthiest people in our country and the discussions are all the same. You cannot out earn or out run your ideas. The road of, "run faster and earn more" will never get you to occupy the land of more than enough time and more than enough money. As long as you and I are breathing, the gap between what we see and what could be will never go away; it will just move.

I know some of you are still not convinced. You're thinking, "Ok, but what about if I was like Warren Buffet rich, Bill Gates rich or Saudi Prince rich? Couldn't I out run my ideas then?" Great question and the Bible actually recounts a story of someone who was even richer than Warren Buffet that put this idea to the test. History tells us that King Solomon was the richest man to ever live. Not only was King Solomon the richest man to ever live, he was one of the wisest men to ever live. Other leaders of the then known world would seek him out and bring him large amounts of wealth and possessions just for the opportunity to glean from his wisdom. Cap that off with the fact that he was the King. So if it was possible to out run or out earn your ideas, Solomon should have been able to do it. So here is what happened when King Solomon set himself to try to out run his ideas. Let's see how it worked out; take a look at his words below:

Ecclesiastes 2:4–11 - [4] I undertook great projects: I built houses for myself and planted vineyards. [5] I made gardens and parks and planted all kinds of fruit trees in them. [6] I made reservoirs to water groves of flourishing trees. [7] I bought male and female slaves and had other slaves who were born in my house. I also owned more herds and flocks than anyone in Jerusalem before me. [8] I amassed silver and gold for myself, and the treasure of kings and provinces. I acquired male and female singers, and a harem[a] as well—the delights of a man's heart. **9** I became greater by far than anyone in Jerusalem before me. In all this my wisdom stayed with me. **10** I denied myself nothing my eyes desired; I refused my heart no pleasure. My heart took delight in all my labor, and this was the reward for all my toil. **11** Yet when I surveyed all that my hands had done and what I had toiled to achieve, everything was meaningless, a chasing after the wind; nothing was gained under the sun.

Ecclesiastes 2:17, 22-23, "So I hated life, because the work that is done under the sun was grievous to me. All of it is meaningless, a chasing after the wind. What do people get for all the toil and anxious striving with which they labor under the sun? **23** All their days their work is grief and pain; even at night their minds do not rest. This too is meaningless."

Inspiring, isn't it? Its amazing that the richest man to ever live, who seemed to have an endless supply of resources, could not out run his ideas. At the end of the day, not only did King Solomon fail to arrive at the land of more than enough by trying to outrun his ideas, but rather a place of anxiety, toil and unfullfillment. King Solomon would later reiterate this truth in Proverbs 23:4 when he said, "Don't wear yourself out trying to get rich, restrain yourself! Riches will disappear in the blink of an eye; wealth sprouts wings and flies away into the wild blue yonder." And here is the reality for you and I, all of us have a gap between what we see and what could be. No matter how much you earn or how fast you run, the gap never goes away; it just moves. Entrepreneurs will always have another business idea and people without business ideas will always have one more thing to go buy. Reality is, most of us will have both because all of us will run out of time before we run out of ideas and opportunities we want to pursue. So, if your definition of being rich is arriving at the place that you have more money than you have ideas, you are searching for a destination that does not exist. You might as well hitch up your boat and head to Big Lake!

Redefining Rich

So what do we do? If culture's definition of being rich is impossible to achieve, what do we do? What do we do with this gap between what we see and what could be? We can't out earn it, we can't out run it. What then, do we do with it? It's like this unhealthy cycle we're in, where we start with all these ideas we want to pursue, many times very noble pursuits. Then we begin this race of trying to outrun or out earn those pursuits and we run and run and run until eventually we fall down from exhaustion. And then we fall into something that is equally as dangerous, exhaustive resignation. Just like Solomon, we say, "Well I give up because I can't seem to ever get to that place were I have outrun my ideas so maybe I just need to give up on pursuing them. I can never seem to get on the other side of the gap between what I see and what could be." It's all vanity and grasping for the wind, right? Here is the good news, you are not sick because you have more ideas than you have time and more ideas than you have money. You are, however, feeling the symptoms of an unhealthy perspective. See, as long as you operated from the conscious or subconscious definition of being rich that says being rich is having more money than I have ideas, you cannot help but look at your gap between what you see and what could be as a problem to be solved. The problem with viewing the gap between what you see and what could be as a problem to be solved is you will spend your entire life in the gap. Therefore, you will be living in a perpetual problem, unable to enjoy the present stage of your journey until you're at the end of it. The problem is you will never be at the end of it on this side of eternity. **The gap between what you see and what could be is actually a gift from God. You cannot help but want to take the environment you are in and make it better because you are hard wired by God to want to do that.** That is why the gap between what we see and what could be never goes away, it just moves. No matter how good your situation, you are built to make it better! I can be content and still have a gap between what I see and what could be. In fact, neither God, nor myself, can be content without a gap because **the gap is the only place faith can live.** *Hebrews 11:1 tells us, "Now faith is the substance of things hoped for, the evidence of things not yet seen." It goes on to say that without faith, it is impossible to please God!* Our wonderful Heavenly Father is a God of adventure and progress, not passivity. From the time God created Adam and Eve, He spoke our gap into existence when He blessed them by saying to them, "Be fruitful and multiply; fill the earth and subdue it; have dominion over the fish of the sea, over the birds of the air, and over every living thing that moves on the earth." What a shame that so many people will never enjoy this wonderful gift of the gap because they look at it as a problem to be solved instead of an adventure to be pursued. It is this gift that allows us to continue to make whatever environment we are in better than what it is and when seen this way we can enjoy the process along the way and find that active rest we all need.

It is in this approach to the gap that we can redefine what it means to be rich. In fact, we can take rich from a noun to a verb. Rich is not a place we arrive at, but rather an activity we engage in. ***Being rich is the activity of creating more than you consume.*** Being rich, the way we define it, is not an attempt to outrun our gap, but rather create more value than we consume right in the middle of it and enjoy the process. **You were built to create more value than you consume in every environment you are in, be it professionally, relationally, physically or financially.** If that is not happening, you will never have the joy and contentment that God hard wired you for. *Proverbs 19:21 advises, "Many are the plans in a man's heart, Nevertheless the Lord's counsel----- that will stand."* Then again in *Proverbs 23:4 it tells us, "Do not over work to be rich, because of your own understanding cease! Will you set your eyes on that which is not? For riches certainly make themselves wings; they fly away like an eagle toward heaven."* It is only when you are fully aware that you have far more ideas than you have time, that you can make the decision to trust and submit to God's priorities for your life. Like God, you have an unlimited ability to dream up ideas to pursue. Unlike God, you have limits on your time and money to pursue them, but these **limits are liberating** because they drive you to pursue the priorities of the One who gave you both your time and money. You can, in essence, enter the active rest of God that Jesus spoke of in Matthew 11:28-30 when he said, "Come to me, all of you who are tired from carrying heavy loads, and I will give you rest. Take my yoke and put it on you, and learn from me, because I am gentle and humble in spirit; and you will find rest. For the yoke I will give you is easy, and the load I will put on you is light. If you have been trying to arrive at extra time and money by out running your ideas, you are carrying a heavy, unsustainable load. Jesus reminds us that the key to rest and margin are found when we live at his limits rather than at the edge of our own capacity. Extra time and extra money are a byproduct of being rich, never the cause of being rich. *Proverbs 21:20 say's –"Wise People live in wealth and luxury, but stupid people spend their money as fast as they get it."* Our only hope to creating more than we consume (in time and money) is by yoking up with God and embracing his priorities for our lives. It is when we pursue God's priorities that we can receive the blessing of the Lord that make us rich. *Proverbs 10:22, "The blessing of the Lord makes one rich, And He adds no sorrow to it."* In the remainder of this book, we will explore how to receive those blessings of the Lord that make us rich. But make no mistake; you have to start by redefining rich. Being rich is the activity of creating more than you consume.

A brief word to the atheist: You thought I was making a lot of sense right up the point I brought God into the equation. I don't blame you for questioning the value of what I write because I have now brought in an element of which you don't believe exists, but I ask you to stay with me in light of the following. If we were to go camping together, and you believed in Bigfoot, and you asked that we prioritize our trek through the woods so as to avoid running into him, I would likely want to protest this logic. However, if once I looked at the proposed trek I found out it would take us to the place I wanted to end up anyway and in fact I would see many more interesting and valuable things along the way, it would be foolish for me to reject the route simply because of your reason for taking it. Also, if you really did believe in Bigfoot and you cared about me, I would expect you do everything you could to help me avoid getting hurt by him. In this way, I am asking you to take a trek with me to the end of the book. Not because you believe in God like I do, but because you will see many interesting and valuable things along the way and I believe end up at the place you wanted to be anyway.

Blowing Up The Money Myth

The great thing about embracing this definition of being rich is it exposes the barriers that have kept us in from being rich for so long and helps us embrace the fundamentals we need to live out this new definition of being rich. Before we move on to the fundamentals, let's deal with a barrier that often stands in the way of any real progress to creating more than we consume.

I love to ask people who are not rich the question, "What do you believe you need to be rich?" In almost 100% of the cases I get some form of the same answer, which pretty much goes like this, "I need more money!" Just like the Gallup pole we looked at earlier, whether a person is making 30K of income a year or 250K of income a year, people who are not rich answer the same way. This myth has stood in the way of millions of people's effort to be rich. This myth causes people to blame the fact that they are not rich on their income, rather than to take responsibility for their choices.

Here is the good news for most of you; income is not the barrier to being rich. Most of you make plenty of money to be rich, you are just not making the choice to create more than you consume. See, under the old definition of being rich, that excuse worked because rich was arriving at the place that you had more income than you had ideas. Being rich meant arriving at the place that you had out earned your gap. As we discussed in the last chapter, that will never happen. You will always have a gap between what you see and what could be. Under the true definition of being rich, you choose to create more than what you consume, with the income you have, right in the middle of the gap. Income is just one reality we have to work with to create more than we consume. The reason most of you are not rich is not because you don't make enough money, it is because you make choices to consume all you create. Therefore, the reason you don't have extra is because you choose to consume your extra. The truth is extra money is a by-product of being rich; it is never the cause. Let's look at a few examples.

One example is lottery winners. How many stories have you heard about the person who was getting by on almost nothing? Then they won 100 million dollar lottery. A few years later that person was bankrupt. Simply Google the words, "the curse of the lottery," and you will have more than a week's worth of reading with such stories. Income was not the problem for these people, they started out with plenty of extra money, and the problem was they did not make the right choices with their extra. That's why Proverbs 20:21 advises an inheritance gained hastily at the beginning will not be blessed at the end. You can give a person a million dollars, but if they do not know how to create more than they consume it will soon be gone. When we are faithful with what we have, then we will be given more. I know what you are thinking, "Yeah, but give me a million and I would be different." Remember, extra money is a by-product of being rich, not the cause. More money will just make you more of what you are. If you are not creating more than you consume with what you have, adding more will simply get you more out of balance than you were before. I understand winning the lottery can feel very far away for most people. So let's look at some examples a little closer to home.

To reiterate, the reason most of you may not feel as though you are rich, is not because you don't make enough money, it is because of the choices you make with your extra. You might say, "But I don't have any extra." Extra is not a function primarily of income, but of the choices we make with our extra. For instance, if you have ever traded in a working something (like a car) for another working something that was just newer, you had extra. You just chose to consume it. If you have ever had a house for your car (you may call it a garage), you had extra. You just chose to consume it. If you ever had to park your car outside because you had to make room for all the stuff you bought that no longer fits in your house, that you no longer use, you had extra. You just chose to consume it. If you have ever sprayed drinking water on your lawn and bought bottled water from the store, you had extra. You just chose to consume it. Now to be clear, none of these decisions are wrong and none of these decisions are off limits to the rich. The key is rich people never make these decisions with their extra. Rich people choose to create more than they consume, rather than consuming all they create. The biggest thing you need to understand here, is they don't have extra because they have run out of ideas for the money, it is because *creating more than they consume has put a perimeter around their behavior when it comes to spending*. Never let income stop you from being rich.

So in summary, being rich is not arriving at the place where you have more money than you have ideas, being rich is the act of creating more than you consume. For most of us, the problem is not money. In fact, most of us make enough money to be rich; we've just never learned how to make the choices that rich people make. We've never learned how to create more than we consume with what we have, so our natural inclination is to think we need more. If we are going to live out this definition of being rich, we can't stop at blowing up the, "I just need more money" myth, we have to embrace the fundamentals.

Fundamental Priorities

NFL head coach Vince Lombardi won five NFL Championships, including Super Bowls I and II, during his tenure with the Green Bay Packers. He was inducted into the Pro Football Hall of Fame in 1971. In the same year, in his honor, the NFL renamed "The Super Bowl Trophy" to the "Vince Lombardi Super Bowl Trophy." What I loved most about Lombardi was his simple dedication to the fundamentals. He was often questioned by other coaches and the media as to what his secret was to building consistently great teams. They all expected to get a very elaborate answer. Vince would simply reply with the following, "Some people try to find things in this game that don't exist, but football is only two things - blocking and tackling." The same thing goes for being rich, people are always looking for things that don't exist. Being rich is about two things, location and direction. King Solomon (the wealthiest man to ever live) said it this way, "Be diligent to know the state of your flocks, and attend to your herds. For riches are not forever, nor does a crown endure to all generations." Now that we have redefined being rich as the activity of creating more than you consume, we can explore what it takes to master the two fundamentals of location and direction in order to live out this definition. Let's take a look at these one at a time.

Part 2 – "You Are Here?"

Location

H ave you ever been physically lost? Sure you have, we all have at one time or another. Whether at an airport, mall, museum, or amusement park, at some point in your life you have been lost. I have the secret as to why you were lost. ---------------Because you didn't know where you were. I know that is not a huge revelation for most of you, but it really is true. The reason we get lost physically is because we don't know where we are. In fact, when most of us get lost what's the first thing we look for to help us get un-lost? The directory, right! And once you find that directory, your eyes begin to scan it for that little red dot that has three very precious words to any lost person, "You Are Here." The reason you and I look for that sticker is because instinctively we know that the reason we are lost is because we don't know where we are. And the first step to getting un-lost is determining our location. You can't get where you want to go until you know where you are. Imagine how foolish it would be to try and get where we wanted to go if we didn't know where we were.

Interestingly the reason we get lost physically is the same reason we get lost financially; we don't know where we are. You can embrace the true definition of being rich (the activity of creating more than you consume) and still fall short of living out that definition if you don't embrace the fundamental of location.

You need the equivalent of a directory and a "you are here" sticker when it comes to two primary financial areas, your assets and your cash flow. This is one area people make a lot of excuses for the fact that they either, don't do this well or don't do this at all. And interestingly the excuses we give, we would not accept if someone managing our money gave them to us, but we accept them in the areas that we have appointed our self as financial advisor. It is also interesting most people who do not really know where they are financially are not all that concerned about it because they don't view this as the problem keeping them from being rich. Most people think the problem is they just need more money. This is the equivalent of being lost in a car and thinking the problem is you just need more gas, when in fact more gas can actually take you further away from where you want to be if you don't know where you are and where you want to go. Through seminars, study groups and one on one meetings, I have had the opportunity to spend time discussing this with thousands of people and here is what I have found to be absolutely true:

1) All of you live off of a percentage of your income.

2) Very few of you know what that percentage is.

As a result, most people are lost financially because they have no regular automated system to find their "You Are Here" sticker on the map of their financial lives when it comes to their assets and their cash flow. Before you remove yourself from this category let me give you some examples of things that indicate you are lost financially.

- If you find yourself repeating the question, "How come we never have any money?" You are lost.

- If you find yourself repeating the question, "Where does all the money go?" You are lost.

- If it takes you more than an hour to calculate your "You Are Here," You are lost.

- If you find yourself saying, "I kind of know what I spend." You are lost.

- If your method of tracking is kept in your head, you are lost.

- If your method is to read your balance off the bottom of the ATM receipt, you are lost.

- If your method is when the bank sends you a letter that you are overdrawn, you are lost.

- If you find yourself saying one of these two statements, "I don't really make enough to keep up with that," or "I make enough not to have to keep up with that." You are lost.

- And my favorite, if you find yourself saying, "That seems like it would take too much time." You are lost.

Isn't it interesting that we will spend 60 or more hours a week working to get more money and push back against spending one hour a week tracking where it all goes. But listen to my words; you cannot be rich if you do not embrace the fundamental of location. You need a "You Are Here Sticker" when it comes to your cash flow and your assets.

Think about how comical this is. If I were your financial advisor and you had been sending me money for six months and you never got any statement, you would probably call me right? Now, can you imagine if when you asked me how your money was doing I responded with any of the following? "You know, I don't really know" or "I don't really keep track of it" or "The problem is you need to send me more" or "I kind of know in my head" or "It would take too much time to keep up with that." How long would I be your financial advisor? So what do you think our heavenly Father is thinking when every week He sends you money and your excuses are the same. The Bible actual informs us, that it is when we are faithful over what we have been given that we will be given more, not the other way around. **You cannot get to where you want to go if you don't know where you are.** All of you live off of a percentage of your income and have assets and liabilities. If you are going to be rich (creating more than you consume), you need a system that quickly and regularly allows you to evaluate where you are financially. **The reason most people cannot create more than they consume is not because they don't create enough,** but because they do not know what's consuming the money they have. They don't know where they are.

Creating and Maintaining Your "You Are Here"

What are the legitimate roadblocks to knowing where you are financially? Most of you at some point did a budget (albeit when you ran out of money) and most of you did a balance sheet (when you were trying to apply for a mortgage). So you may have known where you were at one point in time, but what happened to get you lost again? I think one of the reasons it's easy for us to lose track here is because your "You Are Here" dot is always moving. Banking has become easier and more electronic; literally, as you are sitting here reading this book you likely have electronic drafts and deposits (hopefully more deposits than drafts) that are changing your financial position. If this is the case, why do so many of us fail to automate our tracking and budgeting? Honestly, one of the biggest problems I see when it comes to staying in the habit of knowing were you are, is a lack of automated tracking and budgeting.

When Jamie and I lived in our first home together, we had a very small lawn and no electronic sprinkler system. We didn't want the grass to die so we would water by hand a couple times a week and it seemed to do well. Then as we moved into a bigger home, with a bigger lawn and still no automated sprinkler system (compounded by a really dry summer), watering by hand became too much of a pain so we bought some manual sprinklers that we could move around the yard but still found it to be very time consuming and it often didn't get done and our lawn showed the results of that. Finally, the day came where we got a sprinkler system and automated the process. Oh, it took a while to understand how it worked and it was an investment of money up front, but long term it was and is wonderful. Oh sure, it has to be managed once a week, but in quick fashion I can take note of the health of my lawn and make adjustments to keep it moving in the direction I want. I honestly believe that long term, the more money we make, if we are ever going to be rich we have to invest the time and money in automated tracking and budgeting. The good news here is you don't have to spend thousands on a sprinkler system you can just spend fifty bucks on Quicken. I don't care what you use, provided it automatically links with your bank accounts and it has a budget feature that you can quickly compare how your doing to how you said you would do.

We will talk more about budgeting in a later chapter, but for now if the only thing you did was create an automated way to understand where your money was going, and you looked at it once a week, you would automatically be healthier financially because you would be able to find your "You Are Here" sticker on the directory of being rich. So to get started, here is what I want you to do. Pick a tracking system and track the following four things for at least the next 30 days: Date, what you bought, the category it falls in (miscellaneous is not a category), and how much it cost. We like to refer to this as a "spending blue print," (In the back of the book, there is a Quick Start Guide to get you up and running quickly in this area). At the end of every week I want you to total up the categories you spent money in. You are essentially looking at where the money went and what your assets and liabilities did. I know some of you are saying that's it? Let me tell you a story to show you the power of this.

The Compounding Effect of Daily Decisions

I remember the first time I began to track and categorize my spending. I was young and single and making good money, but surprisingly did not have any left over at the end of every month. I met a financial advisor that challenged me to do this exercise. I remember telling him that tracking wasn't really the problem (after all I balanced my check book), what I needed was more money. He graciously said, "Well humor me and try this because you check book doesn't track all of your spending and it doesn't really categorize any of it." I did it and was shocked. First I was shocked by the amount of money I spent on categories and sub-categories that seemed to be insignificant before I tracked (Starbucks, eating out, entertainment expenses). Now there is nothing wrong with spending money in these areas provided it does not sabotage your other goals that you would consider more important. The second thing that I was shocked by was how just looking at this once a week began to alter the way I spend money in a good way. It was like a weekly reminder that I was going to run out of money before I ran out of ideas and opportunities that I wanted to pursue. And if having extra money (creating more than I consumed) was important to me, I needed to place value on the small daily expenses that seemed to compound by the weeks end. Weekly awareness helps you come face to face with how small daily decisions have a compounding effect over time. This is why if you have ever worked with a personal trainer they have you come in and weigh yourself at least once a week. It creates an awareness of how small daily decisions compound over time either positive or negatively.

So here is the deal, some of you are going to love tracking and categorizing your spending. In fact, while you were reading you were thinking of writing in and giving me tips on better ways than I have described to track and categorize. God bless you; that is how God wired you. However, for most of you this will be a habit you have to create like it was for me. My wife, Jamie, actually likes tracking this stuff. I mean she actually enjoys the process; I just like the result. But I have to encourage those of you who do not enjoy tracking and categorizing that this habit is essential for you to create. Later you can actually pay someone to track it for you and all you have to do is look at it once a week, but until then you need to build this habit into the rhythm of your life. Not doing so is like your boss telling you to be a work at 8:00 and you telling him, "You know I am really not a morning person, I just can't come in at 8:00." There are many things that you have learned to make habits of that were not natural in the beginning. This is not optional if you ever want to be rich or have financial peace. It is mandatory. This is usually the place I get some push back. Someone will say to me, "Well Wes, I am just not wired that way. I am more of the go with flow type; the creative artist type. I just can't see myself doing this every week." Please understand me, I get that and I appreciate that. I benefit from having people in my life that are like you. Listen, some areas of your life you have to harness and resist that and you already know that. You know how I know, because you don't pay your bills that way. You don't call the power company and say, "You know, I am not really a once a month person. I just want to send it in when I feel it, but when I do feel it, I'll also decorate the envelope before sending it in." You would never do that because if you did, you would be decorating the envelope in the dark.

Other side benefit of this is it will reduce the fights that you have with your spouse when it comes to money. Since Jamie and I have been doing this, we have never had a fight about where money went. You know why? Because we eliminate the mystery of where money went because we just pull up Quicken. This is the one area of life there should be no mystery. So many couples end marriages because they fight over accusations like, "It seems like you spend so much money on _____ and it seems like I never get to spend money on anything. This eliminates "it seems like" from the conversation because it either is or it isn't. It is math not philosophy.

The reason people are lost financially is they are so busy trying to get to what could be they don't stop and take inventory of what they see. No amount of money in the world will make you rich if you don't embrace the fundamental of knowing your location. Before we jump to direction I want give you an example of what could happen if you simply embrace this one fundamental of being rich. A few years ago I was introduced to a lady who made pretty good money, was newly divorced, in a lot of debt and thought the answer to her financial problem was she just needed to make more money if she ever hoped to survive. I spent a couple hours with her telling her exactly what I have shared with you so far in this book. Unlike most people who are always talking about stuff and never doing it, she embraced it. And three years later she sent me a letter advising me that she was 100% debt free. Here is what happened:

- *As a result of her divorce she received a huge 5 figure debt from the ex that she did not know existed*

- *Had credit card debt due to the divorce*

- *Still had car & student loans*

- *Had no savings (ready cash)*

- *Was living nearly paycheck to paycheck*

   3 years later

- *Ex husband's debt is paid*

- *Student loan paid off*

- *No credit card debt*

- *Sold home and made a profit*

- *Socked away almost 20% of income each year to savings*

- *Has almost 8 months of savings in ready cash for emergencies*

- *Most perfect credit*

- *Freedom to do more of what she wants*

Jen's situation is a result of her willingness to embrace the fundamental of location. It creates an awareness of how small daily decisions compound over time either positive or negatively. You can't get where you are going if you don't know where you are. Imagine what your situation will look like a year from now if you choose to embrace "You Are Here!"

Part 3 – "Which Way Do We Go?"

Direction

A few years ago I read a great book by Andy Stanley called, "The Principle of the Path." In the book, Andy exposes a fundamental truth when it comes to direction. He says the principle of the path is simply this, "Direction Determines Destination." Not your intentions, not your desire, but your direction determines your destination. For example, lets say I want to go to New York City from my home in Austin, Texas. I can read books about New York, I can talk to others that have been there, I can pray for a safe trip New York and look at maps that will get me there, but if I get on an airplane that heads in a southwest direction I will end up in Mexico not New York. The reason is simple; it is my direction that determines my destination. Every thing else just assists me in determining my direction.

It works the same way when it comes to being rich. I can embrace the real definition of being rich as creating more than I consume. I can get on a tracking and categorization system that helps me know where I am. I can pray about being rich and talk to other people who are rich. But then, every single day make decisions that move me in a direction that is opposite of rich. My direction will determine my destination. So assuming I have done all these other great things, how do I move in the direction of rich instead of not rich? The answer is simple: Prioritizing my pursuits.

Prioritized Pursuits

I once heard a lecture from an Emergency Medical Technician (EMT) that I think really helps bring this to life. He said the most difficult part of training new EMTs came when they taught them how to prioritize the accident scene. "For example," he said, "when we show up on a secured accident site and there are flipped over cars, bloody screaming victims and crying onlookers what do you think most new EMTs want to do first? Without fail most new EMT's instinctively run to those people that scream the loudest." As an audience member, my thought as he said this was, "Well, of course, that just makes sense." Then he said something that shocked everyone. He said, "We teach them to ignore that instinct and go to the screaming people last." Then in dramatic fashion he let that sink in, in absolute silence across the room before he continued. "The reason is simple. The job of the EMT is first and foremost **to save lives**! We are clear about that! And when I pull up onto an accident scene and you are screaming at least I know your breathing. Quite often, my best opportunty to save a life is not the person screaming the loudest, but rather (and he said this part in a slow whisper) *the one dying silently in the ditch.*"

You can embrace the real definition of being rich and the fundamental of location and still move in a direction that is opposite of rich. Not because you don't want to be rich, but because the direction that gets you there doesn't scream very loud. In our effort to grasp every opportunity, we become so busy that we begin to pursue first those opportunities that scream the loudest, while many times our best opportunties die silently in the the ditch. Think about it with me for a miniute. When do most people do a budget? When they are out of money. When do most people start to eat right and exercise? After the heart attack. When do couples start to work on their marriage? When the marriage is in trouble. We could go on and on here, but the reality is in our effort to seize every opportunity we get so busy we tend to pursue those things that scream the loudest while some of our best opportunites go untended. **The unprioritized pursuit of every opportunity will lead you to poverty as surely as the pursuit of nothing at all – just by a different road.** If we are ever going to be rich, the way we defined rich, we have to pursue the right priorities.

Financial Priorities

The major difference between the rich and the not rich are the priorities they pursue. *People do not miss out on being rich because they don't pursue financial priorities, they miss out on being rich because they didn't pursue the right priorities.* For most people the priorities that scream the loudest in their life have to do with getting more money rather than creating more than they consume with what they've already got. The problem with this method of prioritization is it is based on a false assumption that extra money is the cause of being rich. The truth that we spent chapter one uncovering is extra money is a nice by-product of being rich; it is never the cause of being rich. **For most of us the problem is not money. In fact, most of us make enough money to be rich, we've just never learned how to make the choices that rich people make. We've never learned how to create more than we consume with what we have so our natural inclination is to think we need more.** The right priorities will build a perimeter around your daily pursuits and serve as guardrails that keep you moving in the direction of rich. So I will list the priorities and then we will unpack each one. The priorities of the rich are to give 10%, save 10%, and spend the rest elastically. The first priority we will explore is the third priority, elastic spending. I want to be clear, the order of where we send our money should be to give first, save second and spend elastically third, but I know that many people reading this book feel as though they are so far behind right now that giving and saving are just pipe dreams. And until I give you some clarity around how to get healthy, it is difficult for you to hear what I am saying when it comes to giving and saving. My prayer for you is that by the time you get to the end of the book you will see giving and saving as a tool to free you from your current situation, not a governor slowing down your progress.

Elastic Spending

Elastic spending has everything to with the flexibility of the expense you choose. Think of an elastic waistband at Thanksgiving. Before you eat it is small and then after you eat the elastic expands to a new larger size. The good news is, as you lose weight before that beach vacation you don't have to buy new underwear because the elastic waste band contracts to fit your new size. Elastic expands and contracts to fit the environment I create for it.

An elastic spending structure does the same thing; it expands and contracts as the financial environment changes.

The reason this is so important is because our buy-it-now culture baits us toward thinking in terms of payments instead of price. Every time you buy something that requires a long-term monthly payment obligation you have made your spending structure a little less elastic. Let me give you a real life example of how this can sneak up on people who appear to be living within their means.

My CPA told me about two brothers that were in business together. On the surface their income and outgo looked almost identical. They gave 10%, saved 10% and lived off the rest. Because they were fifty-fifty partners in business their gross income was exactly the same. Then the economy changed and their business (though still profitable) could not pay the brothers what it had in previous years. It was at that point that the difference was revealed. One brother had a very elastic spending structure so he was still able to give 10%, save 10% and live off the rest without any major issues. The other brother had a very inelastic spending structure that was committed to many monthly payments that could not easily be taken away. Not only did this brother stop giving and saving, but also he eventually filed bankruptcy giving back many of the assets he was obligated to. In the end, it was not the brothers' income that kept one rich and made the other bankrupt, it was the elastic spending structure.

Bad economies don't create financial problems they just reveal them. In the case of inelastic spending you can make decades worth of decisions that move you in the opposite direction of rich and not even realize there is a problem. The mortgage crisis was a prime example of that. Unlike some other areas of your life, bad spending decisions don't necessarily have immediate negative consequence. I like what Andy Stanley says, "Money doesn't follow the rule of Pinocchio. Remember Pinocchio? Every time he told a lie his nose grew, immediate consequence! If your nose grew every time you made a bad financial decision you would stop making them." But it doesn't work this way, does it? In fact, when I was 19 and I traded in my paid for truck that my parents gave me for my new, far more expensive truck that I financed, my life temporarily got better! I don't even know what the final price I paid was or what my trade in value was because the only thing I cared to negotiate was "the monthlies." I probably don't have to tell you that the weight of inelastic spending decisions has a compounding negative effect. Elastic spending is all about thinking in terms of price instead of payments. Rich people are very careful about maintaining an elastic spending structure.

"But Wes, what if I can earn more on what I have saved than what it costs me to borrow?" I am a financial advisor so I understand this idea, and for many years I subscribed to it. And it took me years to dig out from under it. If you have 30K in an account earning 5% and you can get a loan of 30K at 0%, why would you want to pay cash for it? I mean, if I get into trouble I can always just pay it off. The first reason, I no longer participate in this strategy is we make very different decisions when spending other people's money verses our own. If you had 30K in the bank you are far more considerate about what you choose to spend it on than if you get to keep your 30K and get a new car and a loan. The other reality is very rarely have I seen anyone who doesn't buy far more on credit than what they have in the bank. Because it is easy to spend money you haven't worked to get. But make no mistake every time you do, you take a step into the inelastic and away from being rich.

The reason people fight the idea of thinking in terms of payments instead of price is they don't like to feel like they have to put such tight limits on their spending, but here is the reality, all of us will live at limits, either those we set or those that are set for us by our money and our creditors. The difference between the rich and the not rich is simple, the rich set their own limits and the not rich live by those set for them. *The borrower is slave to the lender*. People who are rich set limits that are liberating by not getting so inelastic that they live under the weight of debt. I am not telling you to never borrow money. I am simply stating that you should be very careful about how much, and for what, you borrow. For the sake of our discussion here the only personal debt that may make sense for you to have is a mortgage that you can put at least 30% down on. And do not do it at the sacrifice of giving or saving. Before you shut this section out, let me ask you a question. Has borrowing money long term made your life better or more complicated? If it has made it better then keep on rolling, if not maybe this is a section you should think about embracing.

Before I move on I want to talk to those who are saying, "Where was this 20 years ago?" I know what it is like to live at financial redline, one paycheck away from disaster. I also know that many of you are buried under the weight of credit card debt, car payments, furniture store payments and mortgages that are too big. I want to give you one simple strategy that when it people do it, it works 100% of the time.

Deleting Debt and Increasing Cash Flow

There are many different debt elimination strategies that companies and people give really cool names and here is what you need to know about choosing one over the other. They are like diets; the one that works the best for you is simply the one you stick to. The strategy I will give you just happens to be the one that is my favorite because I have seen more people stick to it than any other. But if you find one you like better, use it. Never forget the goal is to delete your debt and create an elastic spending structure, any strategy that gets you there works for me. So here we go. List all your debts in order of smallest amount to greatest amount. List the minimum payment next to each even if you are currently paying more than the minimum. Then here is what you will do, pay the minimums on the larger balances and pay as much as you can on the smallest balance until it is paid off. Then take what you were paying on the one you just eliminated and put it all toward the next debt until it is paid off. Repeat this until all your debt is paid off. You might be thinking, what about interest rates, shouldn't I pay off the highest interest rates first? Doesn't that make the most financial sense? This is as much about behavioral economics as anything else. The reason you are in this position in the first place is not because it made financial sense is it? The reason you are in this position is because your emotions prompted you to buy something you couldn't afford to buy unless you thought in terms of payment instead of price. Something powerful happens as you see the quantity of lenders go down as you pay them off. It is using our desire for quick gratification in your favor instead of to your detriment.

The other idea that works well in conjunction with this is to sell stuff, give it away, and pay people to take it away. What stuff you may ask? Start with the stuff you are storing. For example, most of you have no extra money in your savings account but you have a house for your car, (called a garage) that your car can no longer live in because you have to put all the stuff you no longer use in there. Some of you ran out of space in your garage to store the stuff you don't use, so you rented a storage facility you never go to unless you are trying to add more stuff to it. You could sell it, but you would pick up some positive cash flow just by giving it away or even paying someone to take it away (which is sometimes necessary). Call the show hoarders they will pay you to document your journey. This is not only true of little things, but big things too. My wife and I once bought a piece of lake property as an investment (of what not to do). We bought it high and paid on it for five years. The cash burn was about $25K per year for the note, the taxes and HOA fees (not including the large down payment we made on it). Every year we did not sell it at a loss it got harder for us to sell because we felt like we had just stuck another $25K into it. **Sometimes the pain of cashing in on a bad decision keeps us in bondage to that decision, making it worse**. One day we finally looked at each other and said even if we just got away from the note we would be $25K richer a year. The question that really helped us was, "Is the best investment of this $25K a year this property or something else?" The answer was clear; it was something else. Look at where your cash flow is going and ask yourself that question.

Some of you need to sell your house and rent an apartment for a while. Some of you need to sell a car and get something far less expensive.

Example

- Rent A Center	2,000
- Best Buy	4,222
- Home Depot	9,111
- Master Card	10,423
- American Express	11,232
- Car #1	15,278
- Car #2	20,987
- Second Mortgage	30,211
- Mortgage	300,120
Total	**403,584**

The most difficult part of anything new is creating a new habit. It is not an issue of discipline, you are one hundred percent disciplined to your existing set of habits. If you can do the hard work of becoming the steward you were designed to be by God, He is faithful to accelerate the debt eradication process with ways that only God could bring about. My promise to you, in a shorter time than you can fathom today, you will be out of debt and creating more than you consume.

Giving First and Saving Second

This is one of my favorite areas to talk about, particularly to people who aren't doing it. Most people are not against giving and saving, but the priority of their budget is to spend first, then save and give what's left. It's interesting though, there is rarely anything left. And this becomes their reason for not doing it. They mean well, and say things like

"I'll do that when I have extra money." And they look at people who are really good at giving and saving and say to themselves, "Well it's easier for them because they are rich; they have all that extra money. When I have extra money then I'll give and save too." Remember, extra money is never the cause of being rich it is simply a by-product of being rich. Extra money is a by-product of the priorities rich people choose. **Rich people have extra because they choose to prioritize giving and saving before personal consumption.** Thus they are creating more than they consume. They don't give and save because they are out of places to put the money. Remember all of us will run out of time and money before we run out of ideas and opportunities to pursue. Being rich is not about arriving at the place that we have out earned or out run our ideas and then having extra to give and save. Being rich is the activity of creating more than you consume with what you've got right now. Being rich is a verb, not a noun!

Why Save?

This one is generally not all that hard to convince people to do because people like having extra money. The key here is helping them understand that they will always have more ideas than they have money. You will never have extra money if your strategy for getting it is that you will one day reach the place that you have simply run out of ideas to focus your dollars on. Saving is a byproduct of choosing to send money away before you choose to spend it on something. You cannot create more than you consume if you consume more than you create. As we discussed earlier, one of the most difficult parts of saving money is there is rarely any immediate consequences for not doing it. In fact, our life gets temporarily better if

I don't do it in most cases right? Because I get to satisfy my desire to fund an idea, rather than let that idea go unfulfilled. And so, year after year we continue to put spending before savings and now your garage and your $100 per month storage are full of all the ideas you got to fund, but your bank account is empty isn't it? Oh, I am not saying to save every dollar you make. I believe that has devastating effects as well, I am saying to send a minimum of 10% to liquid savings before you spend. The reality is, though there is usually no immediate consequences for choosing to spend before you save, most of you have felt the long-term cumulative effect of not saving. Most people would agree that the reason our country is struggling right now, financially, is because they spent decades ignoring this fundamental principal. The struggle is always that we will rarely change until the money dries up. But let me encourage you. Some of the greatest financial rewards will come to those who learn to embrace the principal of prioritizing saving before they pursue other ideas with their money. In fact, I want to take a look at a story that I think reveals not only the power of this idea but also the time-lessness of it.

Joseph's Example

Economic crises have been happening long before people used the words economic crisis to describe them. The word they used to use was the word famine. For thousands of years because the cultures were very agrarian, famines were used to describe the severe conditions that created a lack of new growth in the earth in the form of produce, which trickled into every area of life. In an environ-ment of famine, not only was there no grain for the people to eat, but no grain for the livestock, which meant no milk, no eggs, no butter and no meat. Therefore, no one is buying, selling or trading, so even if you were not a farmer or a rancher you now have no market for your goods. For instance, if you were a table maker when the famine hit and no one can buy or trade for tables anymore it really doesn't matter how many tables you have in inventory, there was no market to move them. On the other hand, when these same cultures were in what they considered prosperous conditions, there was more than enough produce to keep goods and services changing hands to make up for the fact that no one was storing any of it away. This was what happened in the case of Joseph. Joseph had been brought before Pharaoh to interpret a dream Pharaoh had and then advise him as to what action he should take. Joseph told Pharaoh that he was about to experience seven years of some of the most prosperous conditions they had ever faced and seven years of the most famine like conditions they had ever seen. And Genesis 41:34-36 records the advice he gave Pharaoh in light of this information. "Let Pharaoh do this, and let him appoint officers over the land, to collect one-fifth of the produce of the land of Egypt in the seven plentiful years. And let them gather all the food of those good years that are coming, and store up grain under the authority of Pharaoh, and let them keep food in the cities. Then that food shall be as a reserve for the land for the seven years of famine which shall be in the land of Egypt, that the land may not perish during famine." So picture this, you enter seven very prosperous years, new growth all around. If you had been a farmer your natural inclination when your field produced abundantly was to sell all your grain and either increase your standard of living or (if you are business minded) increase the size of your operation to capture even more opportunity. One way might be to buy another field or two. Meanwhile, the Joseph representing the federal government of the time for Pharaoh, is doing something totally counter to the culture, he's saving 20% of all the produce. Can you imagine how foolish the economist of the day must have thought he was? If there had been television at the time they would have had programs talking about how much more money the government could be making if they would simply take that 20% a year that was sitting idly by and pursue some new investment ideas. And if you had run the numbers at the time you would have seen that the average farmer was outpacing the returns of idle grain by buying another field. Of course, the prices of fields kept going up because you had lots of prosperous farmers willing to keep on buying them. In fact, if you were really smart you would go spend all you have and borrow as much as you could to really leverage up your operation. Or imagine Pharaoh watching all that grain pile up and thinking about all the new ideas he could pursue (for the good of the country of course) if he just sold it. But then (as it always does) the famine hits and it didn't matter how many fields you owned; they weren't producing any thing. And you have to go to the one place that has grain and guess who sets the price of the grain? In a matter of about three years, Pharaoh exchanged his idle grain for all the land, all the livestock and all the money in Egypt and its surrounding areas. The difference between Pharaoh and everybody else was a simple decision to save some of what he created before he reinvested and before he spent. We might not live in an agrarian culture, but the same principle applies today. Extra money is a by-product of choosing to prioritize saving a percentage before spending a percentage.

Why Give?

Why should you give? I mean let's be realistic, from a strictly financial perspective, giving makes no sense if I am trying to create more than I consume, right? If I have ten dollars and I give you one dollar, now I only have nine dollars. That seems to put me further away from rich, doesn't it? And from a strictly financial perspective you would be right. But, there in, lies the issue. Money is not just a financial issue, is it? Money is a spiritual issue.

Billy Graham said, "A checkbook is a theological document, it will tell you who and what you worship. It is very easy, even for those who believe there is a God, to live life with their faith in money, rather than in the God who provides it. This is why the Bible has so much to say about money. Jesus spoke on this dynamic as well, He said, 'No one can serve two masters; for either he will hate the one and love the other, or else he will be loyal to the one and despise the other. You cannot serve God and mammon (your stuff/money)'. This is so interesting because of all the things that Jesus could have said would be in competition for our service, loyalty and love when it comes to our relationship with God, He chose to identify money as the key competitor for our hearts.

The Gallup Pole we looked at earlier is a great indicator, that by default when it comes to being rich, most people put their faith in their money rather than in the blessings of their God that Proverbs 10:22 says makes one rich without sorrow. Any time you and I begin to operate as if more money is the answer to our financial problems, we have shifted our devotion away from God. 1 Timothy 6:10 advises, "For the love of money is a root of all *kinds of* evil, for which some have strayed from the faith in their greediness, and pierced themselves through with many sorrows." It is very easy to look at our money as the key to the rest we all seek, but doing so is the equivalent of putting our faith in money's ability to make us rich rather than God's. God wants you to be rich, but putting your faith in money's ability to get you there only leads to great sorrow. God is not against you having money; He's against your money having you. We often laugh as we read the Old Testament stories of people serving wooden or gold statues, but if we looked at your calendar and your check-book, what would it reveal that you are serving? It might not be a statue, but it could easily be a bunch of green pieces of paper with dead presidents on them.

Any time our faith is in our money we are fueled by the power of greed. Greed is almost impossible to see in the mirror. **Greed is simply the assumption that whatever I have is for my consumption.** The spirit of greed will never lead you to be rich it will only lead you to be tired. God knows this would be a though issue for us to wrestle with. That's why over and over again in His word he talks about the one thing that breaks the power of greed in our lives, the power of generosity.

Generosity keeps the stuff I own from owning me. Generosity, out of faith in God, opens the door for God to get supernaturally involved in my finances. In fact, Solomon eventually figured this out and said it this way in Proverbs 11:24-25, "One person gives freely, yet gains even more; another withholds unduly, but comes to poverty. A generous person will prosper; whoever refreshes others will be refreshed."

I remember when I first came face to face with this principal I heard my pastor, Rob Koke, teach on what God said about money. He was teaching from an Old Testament scripture in Malachi 3:9-12. Now before I get into that section of scripture, I want to take a minute to address one of the most common responses to the idea of giving tithes and offerings. If you are a Christian and you struggle with giving, your natural response is to look for reasons not to have to do it. For instance, if I teach you about giving by reading the Old Testament you might say, "Yea Wes, but that is Old Testament. That was when we were under the law and the

Ten Commandments. We are under grace now." Or, you might say something like a friend of mine said one day on this topic, "Wes, Corinthians tells, 'Let each person give according to their own heart, not under compulsion, but willingly. For God loves a cheerful giver.' And Wes, I think I am a lot more cheerful if I get to keep my money!" I understand where you are coming from, but just hear me on two things that remove the barriers that arguments create.

First, it is never wise to use New Testament grace to lower your operating standard below that of the Old Testament law. In fact, Jesus himself taught on this as he compared pieces of the Old Testament law with the new standard that grace makes possible. In Matthew 5 He said, "You've heard it said, 'do not murder,' but I say if you hate your brother you have already committed murder in your heart." Then again he said, "You've heard it said, 'do not commit adultery', but I say if you look at a woman and lust after her you have already committed adultery in your heart." So to use the empowering grace of the New Testament to lower your standard below that of the Old Testament law is contrary to what Jesus taught. The standard goes up when you are operating out of grace, not down.

Second, Jesus himself in the New Testament said that we should tithe! In Matthew 23:23 He said, "Woe to you, scribes and Pharisees, hypocrites! For you pay tithe of mint and anise and cumin, and have neglected the weightier *matters* of the law: justice and mercy and faith. These you ought to have done, without leaving the others undone." Jesus was saying we should tithe, as well as focus on all the other stuff the word teaches. The reality of giving is, it is not a free pass to ignore everything else God has to say about money (as I will show you in a personal story later on). God is a good Father, and He wants to build in us the capacity to receive the blessings that make us rich. Breaking the power of greed through being generous toward God is a key fundamental to building that capacity.

So anyway, back to when this idea of giving came alive in my life. My pastor was teaching out of Malachi 3:9-12, "You are cursed with a curse, for you have robbed Me, *Even* this whole nation. Bring all the tithes into the storehouse, that there may be food in My house, and try Me now in this," Says the LORD of hosts, "If I will not open for you the windows of heaven and pour out for you *such* blessing that *there will* not *be room* enough *to receive it.* And I will rebuke the devourer for your sakes, so that he will not destroy the fruit of your ground, nor shall the vine fail to bear fruit for you in the field," Says the LORD of hosts; "And all nations will call you blessed, for you will be a delightful land," Says the LORD of hosts. I remember hearing this and thinking, I am scared to do this and I don't understand it, but I am going to choose to put my faith in what God can do with my 90% rather than what I could do with 100%. After a quick marital adjustment session (or fight) with Jamie, we began to give away 10% of all our income first. God was faithful to honor His word. Not only did we never lack what we needed, but because our hearts follow where we put our treasure, we began to see the world through the lens of generosity and abundance. We began to embrace the other things the word of God said about money and operate accordingly. Today, we give away far more than we used to make, and still have left over time and left over money. I can tell you this scripture has not only come alive, but has come to take on a much deeper meaning in our lives. See, I used to read Malachi as if God was saying we were robbing him of money. What I have come to see is we were really robbing

God of the opportunity to be involved in our provision. Generosity, out of faith in God, not only breaks the miserable existence of serving money, but releases God to move on your behalf in the area of your finances. As Solomon said, "The world of the generous gets larger and larger; the world of the stingy gets smaller and smaller. The one who blesses others is abundantly blessed; those who help others are helped." I have so many giving stories to share that I could make a separate book out of them. Maybe one day I will, but until then let me share just a few.

I remember early on in my business after we had been tithing for a few years and our church was raising money to build a state of the art children's facility. Jamie and I really felt as though God was impressing on our hearts to commit two thousand dollars a month to the project for the next three years in addition to our tithe. This was a giant step of faith for us because the previous year our gross income was $124,000. Our tithe and offering was about $16K. Once we paid all our business expenses and personal expenses, there just wasn't an extra $24K to go around. In the natural this didn't make sense. We started asking ourselves was it really God that put this on our hearts or was it the pizza we ate last night? In the face of enormous anxiety, we began sending our $2K a month in addition to our tithe. For the next eight months we saw our personal savings dwindle and my business line of credit stack up to its maximum of $75K (this was before I learned about elastic spending). It was in this environment that we began to search God's word and see that we were living out of balance financially in many other areas. In fact, much of what you have read in this book came out of that time. Even though we were tempted to quit giving, we knew that God was using this time to mold us in a container that could receive the blessings he had for us. Just like I would never give a car to my five year old, our heavenly Father doesn't want to give us something we are not ready for yet. Proverbs 20:21 says, "An inheritance gained hastily at the beginning will not be blessed at the end." If we had immediately been given more financial increase without going through the period of testing, that blessing would have run right through our fingers. It's amazing how motivated you are to change when the money dries up. And if we were wrong and had missed God, we made the decision to err on the side of generosity and faith rather than succumbing to our fears. I want to be clear we still worked really hard to make the other changes we believed the word of God was leading us to. Yes, we still kept giving, but we also made the other in course corrections along the way. Then in months 9, 10 and 11 things began to turn around when we had our first profitable months since we had made the commitment. But it was in month twelve that the supernatural blessing of God that blew us away. Out of the blue, a man that I had known through a bible study we both participated in came up to me and said, "I have been watching you for some time. I have sold my business and have a substantial amount of money that I need you to take care of for me." Three weeks later we completed the largest engagement of my career and the proceeds were not only enough to restore everything that we had spent down and the debt I had incurred, but to leave us with $50K extra. Looking back, if that case had come in the beginning of the year instead of the end, I honestly believe I would not have learned the lessons that I am conveying to you today.

Another great story I think about had to do with my operations director, Stephanie, when she came to work for me years ago. I had needed a person to replace my assistant that was leaving and thought I had found them, when the Friday before they were supposed to come to work they called to say they couldn't take the job. Since my existing assistant was leaving it put me in a real bind. I took the weekend to pray about it and as I was journaling on Saturday afternoon, when out of the blue I wrote the words, "Hire Brian's assistant." Now this seemed particularly odd to me since I had never met Brian's assistant and Brian was my friend and I couldn't imagine that stealing her away was the right thing to do. Nevertheless on Monday morning, as I was telling David, another mutual friend of Brian's and mine, about my predicament, he said, "Well have you thought about hiring Brian's assistant?" To which I said, "Tell me more." As it turns out, due to some personal issues, Brian's assistant, Stephanie, needed full time work. She had been interviewing with a few firms and was going to make a decision by the end of that day to go with one of them. I went to Brian's office and met her and explained my need for a new executive assistant. We had a quick interview and even though she wanted a little higher starting pay then what I had planned for I thought she would be a great fit. After a quick conversation with my wife, I called Stephanie and gave her the job. Now, as Paul Harvey says, "The rest of the story." Due to a divorce, Stephanie as a single mom of two found that a part time income would no longer cover her bills. As she began to explore what the full-time work opportunities available to her would pay, she would be basically breakeven. Breakeven that is, if she chose not to tithe the first ten percent of her income. That Saturday afternoon, she was faced with a choice, to live by faith or the consequences of her doubt. As she sat down to pay the bills, she made a decision to trust God and wrote the tithe check in spite of what seemed like a no win situation. By the way, just in case you forgot, it was Saturday afternoon when I wrote the words, for no apparent reason, "hire Brian's assistant" in my journal. What I would agree to pay her was exactly what she would need to tithe, pay bills and still have positive cash flow left over. I believe that as she moved her hand to write her tithe check that Saturday afternoon that God moved my hand to write "hire Brian's assistant." Supernatural economics are always better than natural economics.

One more story and then we will close. Jamie and I had been saving to build our dream home on a plot of land that we had been paying on for several years. After looking at all the costs associated with it we did not feel comfortable moving forward on the construction loan until we saved about double what we had, which we knew would take some time. Then shortly after we had gone through this fact-finding process a close friend of ours lost his job. Unable to find work near what he was making before, he got behind on his car payments and they repossessed the car. It was then that I felt as though God was going to supply them with a car that was paid for. The problem was I got the sneaking suspicion he wanted to do it through Jamie and I. After we talked about it, we knew that we needed to get them a car. So we took $13K that we had set aside for the house and bought them a car. It was one of the greatest joys of our lives. See, God is in the business of miracles but he uses people to hand them out and we knew that for this family at that time we were giving them a miracle. About six months later I got a call from the FDIC. They had taken over our loan on the land we wanted to eventually build our house on because the original bank had gone under. The controller for the FDIC said, "Mr. Young, we are getting ready to sell your loan to another bank. We would like to give you the opportunity to buy it out first. We are willing to offer you a discount of 10% if you can come up with the money in the next month and a half." I said, "Wow, you are going to give me 10% off my loan if I bring you the cash to pay it off." He said, "Actually, if you can bring cash in the next two weeks we will give you 15% off." I told him it was a deal and that I would get the money together and get back with him the following week. There was just one problem. I owed $140K on the land. A 15% discount would take $21K off that price so I would owe $119K. I did not have $119K that I could get in the next two weeks, but I had a God. It wasn't long until a friend of mine called me for some unrelated reason and asked me how things were going. I relayed the FDIC story to him, but did not tell him I needed any money, and then we moved on to talk about other things. Now keep in mind he didn't know what my financial situation was, but just before we hung up the phone he said, "Hey, just let me know if you need me to wire you any money to get that FDIC deal done." Within two days he had $100K dollars wired to my account without even a contract and I got the deal done. One year later building costs had come down so much we were able to start construction on our dream home where we live today. Supernatural economics are way better than natural economics.

Giving is not a magic wand. God wants you to be a faithful steward over all the money that comes your way not just the first ten percent. But make no mistake giving begins the process of allowing God to get supernaturally involved in your finances. Giving breaks the power of greed and focuses you on preparing yourself to receive the blessing of God that makes one truly rich.

You have a choice of what you will do with what you read. You can put your faith in the Provider or the provision. I encourage you to take the first ten percent and give it to God through your church. By doing so, you will release His hand in your financial life. How silly would it be to trust God with your eternal salvation, but not with the money that he sends your way in the first place? Remember

Proverbs 10:22 tells us, "The blessings of the Lord make one rich, and he adds no sorrow with it." Position yourself to receive the blessings of the Lord and see his supernatural provision in your life.

<u>Wrap Up</u>

In closing, being rich is not arriving at the place that you have more money than you have ideas. Being rich is the act of creating more than you consume. For most of us the problem is not money. In fact, most of us make enough money to be rich, we've just never learned how to make the choices that rich people make. We've never learned how to create more than we consume with what we have, so our natural inclination is to think we need more. The path to creating more than you consume begins by redefining being rich as the activity of creating more than you consume. The two fundamentals you must master to live out that definition are location and direction. Location is all about knowing where your money is going and direction is about giving first, saving second and elastic spending. The path is clear and the choice is yours.

Quick Start Guide

<u>From Busy to Rich</u>

B eing rich is not arriving at the place that you have more money than you have ideas. Being rich is the act of creating more than you consume. For most of us the problem is not money, in fact most of us make enough money to be rich we've just never learned how to make the choices that rich people make. We've never learned how to create more than we consume with what we have, so our natural inclination is to think we need more. The path to creating more than you consume begins by redefining being rich as the activity of creating more than you consume. The two fundamentals you will need to master to live out this definition are location and direction. Location is all about knowing where your money is going and direction is about giving first, saving second and elastic spending. The path is clear and the choice is yours.

Practical Application

Use the spending blueprint template as it best suits the season of life you are in. For instance, many people use it as a template to set up their budget in Quicken or some similar personal finance program. Others use it as a format to make their own spreadsheets and some make hard copies and write directly on the paper. My experience has been that for a budget to work long term (and as effectively as possible) it becomes critical to use it inside of a Quicken-like system (especially as incomes get larger).

The template is made up of master categories and subcategories. The subcategories of each master category are samples to get your mind thinking of all the things you spend money on. Please customize them to fit your life. However, refrain from altering the master categories or the order they are in. Let me break them down for you as you use the budget template as a reference.

1. *Income* – Money that is coming into your control from all sources.

2. *Giving* – Giving back a piece of what has been entrusted to your care.

3. *Saving* – Putting away for the opportunities or unexpected things you cannot yet see. If you own a business this will be the place you also store the money you owe in taxes.

4. *Fixed Expenses* – Expenses that are going to be there month in and month out that do not fall into the other two expense categories.

5. *Inelastic Expenses* – These are inelastic expenses created by things you've bought with someone else's money (typically a bank's money). This will be the place you use your debt reduction strategy as mentioned in Part Three of the book.

6. *Fluctuating Expenses* – Expenses that will be impacted drastically in one direction or another depending on the mood you are in. For instance, if I go to the grocery store hungry I will spend far more than if I am full.

The reason it is important to keep them in this order is because most people are living in reverse. They spend first with the intention of giving and saving if there is anything left. There never is anything left. The order is important because you are telling the money where it will go before it goes.

You will notice the percentages listed next to each category on your spending blueprint template. These are there to help give you an idea as to the starting standard to shoot for. In the beginning, you may find you do not have enough income to contribute the minimum desired percentages listed next to the categories and still pay all of the expenses you have committed to. Let me encourage you to ask the right questions at this point, instead of prophesying your defeat. What I mean by this is don't say, "Well we just can't do it." Ask instead, "How can we get there?" Starting with the bottom up, ask yourself, "In light of where we are for this season, what do we believe is appropriate for us to be spending on in this category?" This may be another good time to run your numbers by a trusted advisor and then have ears to hear what they say you should do. As a last resort, you may have to point money from savings and investing for a time to credit cards or some other financed expense. Notice I did not say take money from your Giving.

Ok, I have given you enough overview to get you to the place that you should now be able to follow the basic instructions from the budget template worksheet and get started.

Spending Blueprint Quick Start Instructions

Step (1)
Read the Book "From Busy to Rich"

Step (2)
Input the numbers for your Location Column *(What you* spent **last** *month)*

Step (3)
Create the numbers for your Direction Column *(What you want to spend this month)*
1. Input Giving and Saving numbers at 10%
    Note: After you adjust all your expenses you may have to come back and temporarily alter your savings while you get the rest of your expenses in line. But Save Something. Also. I urge you to not alter the Giving, as we want God's hand Involved. (see Why Give? Section of the book)

2. Analyze all current fixed expenses and ask yourself two questions, How can I do belter or spend less? Am I willing to that to get to my desired situation? Make appropriate changes to the Direction column.

3. Analyze Inelastic expenses and ask yourself, What debt do I want to focus on eliminating first? (use the debt reduction plan discussed in the book) List the changes for the month in the Direction column.

4. Analyze fluctuation expenses and ask yourself the following, In light of my spending blueprint above. what is reasonable for me to spend in these categories? Am I wiling to spend reasonably in these categories?

Step (4)
Consider going to a cash spending strategy for all fluctuating expenses. Pick a weekly date to review the results and to pull out cash for tile next week. **(Log this date in your day planner as a must do.)**

Step (5)
Set a monthly date to review your Direction column (what you planned to do) V.S. your Results Column (what you actually did) and then start at step 1 for the new month. **(Log this date In your day planner as a must do.)**

Spending Blueprint Template (personal)

Income	Personal Income	Reality	Revision	Results
Income	Salary			
	Bonus			
10% Giving	**Tithes & Offerings**			
	Tithes			
	Offerings			
	Other Charity			
10% Savings	**Savings**			
	Savings Accounts			
	Other Savings			
	CVLI			
80% Elastic Spending	**Fixed Expense**			
	Phone			
	Cable			
	Gas			
	Water			
	Electric			
	Cell phone			
	Doctor			
	Internet			
	Health Ins.			
	Car Ins.			
	Term Life Ins.			
	Hair cut			
	Clothes			
	Vacation			
	Car Service			
	Inelastic Expense			
	Mortgage/ Rent			
	Car Payment			
	Credit Card			
	Fluctuating Expense			
	Groceries			
	Spending Husband			
	Spending Wife			
	Entertainment Together			
	Total Expenses			
	Total Remainder			

This book is dedicated to my wife Jamie.

You are a gift from God.

W ESLEY YOUNG is the founder of the financial consulting firm

Wes Young & Associates.Wes specializes in helping business

owners build profitable, sustainable business operations. In addi-

tion to working with private clients, he has served on the board

of advisors to some of the nations largest privately held compa-

nies. He is an author and speaker, receiving invitations to teach at

churches, financial forums, business groups and leadership con-

ferences all across the country. Many have benefited from his

audio and video teaching as well as his books. Wes and his wife,

Jamie, live in Austin, Texas with their children Gage and Abby.

Made in the USA
San Bernardino, CA
12 May 2017